OUR AMAZING CONTINENTS

Continents are the largest pieces of land on Earth. There are seven continents. The largest is Asia. The other continents, from largest to smallest, are Africa, North America, South America, Antarctica, Europe, and Australia. Each continent's landscape has shaped the lives of its animals, plants, and people.

Library of Congress Cataloging-in-Publication Data

Sayre, April Pulley.
South America, surprise! / April Pulley Sayre.
p. cm.—(Our amazing continents)
Summary: Introduces the continent of South America, looking at its
geography, plant and animal life, weather, and settlement by humans.
ISBN 0-7613-2123-3 (lib. bdg.)
1. South America—Juvenile literature.   2. Natural history—South
America—Juvenile literature.   [1. South America.]   I.Title.
F2208.5.S292   2003
918—dc21   2002151310

Front cover photograph courtesy of Bruce Coleman, Inc. (© Erwin & Peggy
Bauer); Back cover photograph courtesy of Bruce Coleman, Inc. (© Stuart
D. Klipper)

Photographs courtesy of NASA: p. 1; Woodfin Camp & Associates: pp. 3
(© Mireille Vautier), 11 (bottom: © Robert Frerck), 13 (top: © Geoffrey
Clifford), 16-17 (© Loren McIntyre), 22-23 (© Stephanie Maze);
Photo Researchers, Inc.: pp. 4 (© Jeff Greenberg), 12 (© Dr. Morley
Read/SPL), 17 (top: © Gregory Ochocki), 29 (left: © Victor Englebert), 31
(left: © Ellan Young); Animals Animals/Earth Scenes: pp. 5 (top left: © Joe
McDonald; top right: © E. R. Degginger; bottom: © M. Gibbs/OSF), 14 (©
Fabio Colombini), 15 (bottom: © Patti Murray), 19 (top: © Howie Garber:
middle: © Erwin & Peggy Bauer; bottom: © Dani/Jeske), 20 (© Fabio
Colombini), 23 (bottom: © Fabio Colombini), 25 (© Barbara Reed), 31
(bottom right: © Nigel J. H. Smith); Corbis: pp. 6 (© Carol & Ann Purcell),
11 (top: © Peter Guttman), 24 (bottom: © Adam Woolfitt), 28 (© Peter
Guttman), 29 (right © Hubert Stadler), 30 (© Paul Almasy), 31 (top right:
© Dave G. Houser); Bruce Coleman, Inc.: pp. 7 (© Frank Krahmer), 13
(bottom: © Erwin & Peggy Bauer), 15 (top: © Joachim Messerschmidt), 17
(bottom: © John Giustina), 18 (© Fulvio Eccardi), 21 (© Francisco Erize), 23
(top: © Erwin & Peggy Bauer), 24 (top: © Tui De Roy), 26 (© Guido
Cozzi), 27 (all: © Guido Cozzi); Photri, Inc.: p. 8; National Geographic
Image Collection: p. 10 (© Louis O. Mazzatenta)

Published by The Millbrook Press
2 Old New Milford Road
Brookfield, CT 06804

Farmlands in the valleys of
the Andes Mountains, Peru

SOUTH AMERICA, SURPRISE!

APRIL PULLEY SAYRE

THE MILLBROOK PRESS, BROOKFIELD, CONNECTICUT

Giant Galápagos tortoise

Where can you find giant anteaters and giant tortoises?

Where can you see fish swimming among flooded trees?

Where can you see parrots, piranhas . . . and penguins?

In South America.

anteater

White-bellied parrot

Wimple piranha

South America is full of surprises.

Trinidad

The continent of South America is connected to North America.

The top of South America is connected to North America. The border is between two countries: Colombia and Panama. Colombia is in South America. Panama is not. It is in Central America and is part of the North American continent.

South America stretches almost all the way to Antarctica. The southern tip of South America is called Cape Horn. It is about 600 miles (1,000 kilometers) from Antarctica.

Elephant seals and Magellanic
penguins on Cape Horn

South America is mostly in the Southern Hemisphere.

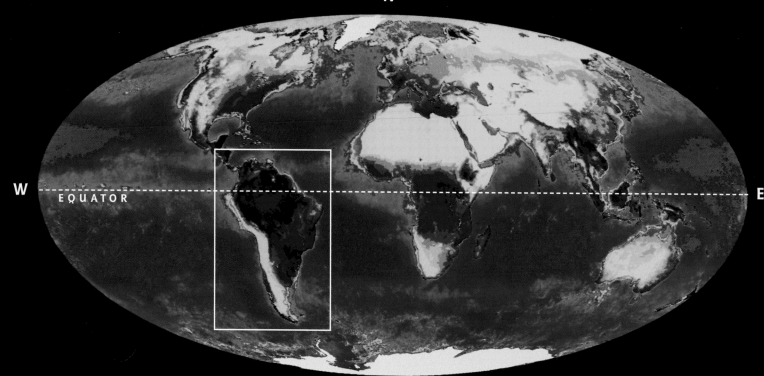

N

W

EQUATOR

E

S

The Southern Hemisphere is the area south of the equator. The equator is an imaginary line that circles Earth's middle, like a belt. The South American country of Ecuador is on the equator, and is named for it. South America begins just north of the equator and stretches far into the Southern Hemisphere.

Places that are near the equator are generally warmer than those farther away. So, the northern countries of Ecuador and Colombia have warm weather, except for high in the mountains. Patagonia, an area near the southern tip of South America, is colder. It has glaciers and penguins.

Like Australia, the southern part of South America has seasons that occur at the opposite time of those in North America.

For instance, summer in Patagonia is in December and January. July is wintertime!

South America has many countries.

Cowboys, known as gauchos, in Argentina

A day to play in Suriname

A continent is not a country. A country is an area ruled by a government. South America's mainland has 12 countries: Argentina, Bolivia, Brazil, Chile, Colombia, Ecuador, Guyana, Paraguay, Peru, Suriname, Uruguay, and Venezuela.

French Guiana is a region of South America that is ruled by France, even though France is far away, in Europe.

Sunday market in Pisac, Peru

This active volcano releases hot gases and ash.

The Andes Mountains line South America's western side.

The Andes is the second-tallest group of mountains on Earth. (The Himalayas, in Asia, are the tallest.) The highest mountain peak in the Andes is Aconcagua, in Argentina.

Many of the mountains in the Andes are active volcanoes. They are part of the Ring of Fire, a group of volcanoes that forms a circle around the Pacific Ocean.

Rock formations

When the Andean volcanoes erupt, the snowcaps on their peaks melt, forming water that mixes with dirt, causing mudslides. These volcanoes also spurt out gas and lava.

Vicuña and guanacos live in the Andes. They are the wild relatives of llamas and alpacas.

Guañaco

To the east are highlands and famous waterfalls.

Highlands are just what you might guess: high land. But highlands are not steep and pointed like mountains. South America's highlands are like gigantic bumpy tables. There are two groups of highlands: the Guiana highlands and the Brazilian highlands.

Highlands

Iguaçu Falls

Waterfalls spill over the edges of the highlands. One such waterfall is Angel Falls, the world's highest waterfall. Another beautiful sight is Iguaçu Falls. Iguaçu means "big water." Iguaçu Falls has over two hundred different water-falls. Rainbows often form in its mists.

Angel Falls

Between the Andes and the highlands are lowlands and the Amazon River.

The Amazon River holds more water than any other river on Earth.

The Amazon River dolphin, also called a pink dolphin

Giant otter

Amazon River

Three rivers drain South America's lowlands: the Río de la Plata, the Orinoco, and the Amazon. The Amazon River is the second longest on Earth. (The longest is the Nile.)

Over 1,300 species of fish live in the Amazon River. River dolphins and giant otters live in the Amazon River, too.

Rain forest

Surrounding the river is the Amazon rain forest.

The Amazon rain forest is Earth's largest rain forest. It is rainy and wet.
It has tall trees. It has many different kinds of plants and animals. Tapirs, jaguars,
monkeys, macaws, and iguanas live in the rain forest.

Some parts of the forest flood after heavy rains.

Fish swim among tree branches. Some eat fruit from the flooded trees. Sloths swim from tree to tree. After several months, the water level goes down. Then, animals that left the flooded area can return.

Pair of macaws

Jaguar

Sloth

Rhea with chicks

The lowlands are also filled with grasslands and savannas.

Cowboys herd cattle in South America's famous grasslands: the llanos and the pampas. These cowboys are called "gauchos" or "llaneros." Giant anteaters and huge birds called rheas wander the wilder parts of South America's grasslands.

Anteater investigating a termite mound

Some of South America's grasslands are savannas. Savannas have grass but also scattered bushes and trees. Termites build large mounds on the savannas. Giant anteaters eat the termites.

South America has wetlands.

Birds get a ride through the swamp on the capybaras.

Caiman

The Pantanal

Wetlands are areas covered by water all or part of the year. The Pantanal, Earth's largest wetland, is in the lowlands. Herds of capybaras, which are giant rodents, roam the Pantanal. Marsh deer, caimans, and large flocks of herons, egrets, and storks live in the Pantanal as well.

South America has beautiful seashores and islands.

South America has many islands, such as Aruba, Bonaire, Curaçao, Trinidad, Tobago, the Juan Fernández Islands, and the Galápagos Islands. The Galápagos Islands are part of Ecuador. Giant tortoises and large iguanas live in the Galápagos. Seabirds such as albatrosses and blue-footed boobies nest on the islands.

Galápagos tortoises in a pond formed in the center of an inactive volcano

Net fishing in Trinidad

Iguanas soak up the sun on a rocky island.

A small oasis in the Atacama

Along one shore is the Atacama Desert.

Not many people live in the Atacama.

The Atacama Desert is on the coast of Chile. The Atacama is cool and dry.

It is so dry that sometimes rain does not fall there for twenty years.

Fog from the Pacific Ocean blows inland, but the land still remains dry.

The Atacama at the foothills of the Andes

Desert fox

Flamingos fly over the desert.

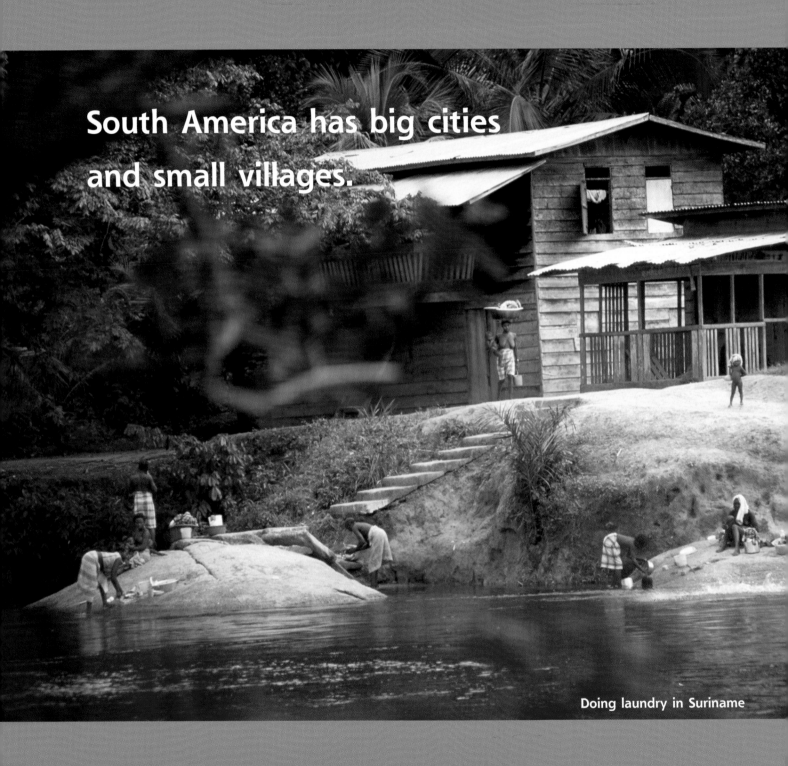

South America has big cities
and small villages.

Doing laundry in Suriname

South America has large cities such as Rio de Janeiro, São Paulo, and Buenos Aires. Most of South America's large cities are along the coasts. Yet South America also has small villages, only reachable by hiking or by canoe. A tribe of Indians called the Yanomamo has lived deep in the Amazon jungle for thousands of years, and still lives there today.

Christmas in Buenos Aires

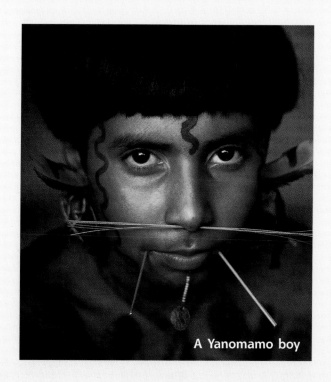
A Yanomamo boy

South America has many different customs.

Children in Chile

Bolivia

Tobago

Most South Americans speak Spanish or Portuguese. But there are many other languages spoken by small groups, in local areas. Food, clothing, cultures, and customs vary from place to place. South America's large cities are full of people who have come from all over the world. They share their customs with one another. South America has wonderful surprises, for people who look and listen for them.

Brazil

SOUTH AMERICA

NORTH
AMERICA

Caribbean Sea

ATLANTIC
OCEAN

Orinoco River

COLOMBIA

Galápagos
Islands

Angel Falls

Guiana
Highlands

ECUADOR

Equator

Amazon River

Ring of Fire

ANDES MOUNTAINS

Atacama Desert

Brazilian
Highlands

Pantanal

Iguaca Falls

Mt. Aconcagua

PACIFIC
OCEAN

Rio de la Plata

PATAGONIA

Cape Horn

KEY
Highlands
Lowlands
Desert
Pampas
Steppe
Rain Forest

0   600 miles

0   900 kilometers

How do you get to know the face of a continent?

Books are one way. This book is about the natural features of a continent. Maps are another way. You can discover the heights of mountains and the depths of valleys by looking at a topographical map. A political map will show you the outlines of countries and locations of cities and towns.

Globes are a third way to learn about the land you live on. Because globes are Earth-shaped, they show more accurately how big the continents are, and where they are. Maps show an Earth that is squashed flat, so the positions and sizes of continents are slightly distorted. A globe can help you imagine what an astronaut sees when looking at our planet from space. Perhaps one day you'll fly into space and see it for yourself! Then you can gaze down at the brown faces of continents, and the blue of the oceans, and the white clouds floating around Earth.